FIRST AMERICANS
The Menominee

SARAH De CAPUA

Marshall Cavendish
Benchmark
New York

ACKNOWLEDGMENTS

Series consultant: Raymond Bial

Marshall Cavendish Benchmark
99 White Plains Road
Tarrytown, New York 10591
www.marshallcavendish.us

Text, maps, and illustrations copyright © 2010 by Marshall Cavendish Corporation
Map illustrations by Rodica Prato
Craft illustrations by Chris Santoro

Library of Congress Cataloging-in-Publication Data
De Capua, Sarah.
The Menominee / by Sarah De Capua.
p. cm. — (First Americans)
Includes index.
Summary: "Provides comprehensive information on the background, lifestyle, beliefs, and present-day lives of the Menominee people"—Provided by publisher.
ISBN 978-0-7614-4131-1
1. Menominee Indians—History—Juvenile literature. 2. Menominee Indians—Social life and customs—Juvenile literature. I. Title.
E99.M44D39 2008
977.4004'97313—dc22
2008041999

Front cover: A Menominee boy attends the Annual Gathering of Nations Powwow in Albuquerque, New Mexico.
Title page: A colorful sample of Menominee beadwork
Photo research by: Connie Gardner
Cover photo by Michael De Freitas

The photographs in this book are used by permission and through the courtesy of: The photographs in this book are used by permission and through the courtesy of: *Nativestock*: Marilyn "Angel" Wynn; 1, 17, 31, 36; *Alamy*: Bidagentur-on line McPhoto-ERD, 26; Northwind, 7; *Northwind Picture Archives*: 8, 16, 34; *Corbis*: Bettmann, 11, 13, 19, 29; Richard Hamilton Smith, 14; *Getty Images*: Hulton Archive, 21, 39; Gary Vestal, 33; *AP Photo*: Donna Hobscheid, 41.

Editor: Deborah Grahame
Publisher: Michelle Bisson
Art Director: Anahid Hamparian
Series Designer: Symon Chow

Printed in Malaysia
1 3 5 6 4 2

CONTENTS

MENOMINEE HOMELAND

CANADA

Ontario

Quebec

Lake Superior

Minnesota

Menominee River

Wisconsin

MENOMINEE

Green Bay

Lake Huron

Lake Michigan

Fox River

Lake Winnebago

Lake Ontario

Mississippi River

Wisconsin River

New York

Michigan

Lake Erie

Des Moines River

Iowa

Pennsylvania

Missouri River

N

Illinois

Indiana

Ohio

West Virginia

Kansas

Missouri

Kentucky

Virginia

0   100   200   300 mi

- 1 · WHO ARE THE MENOMINEE PEOPLE?

Members of the Menominee (meh-NOHM-uh-nee) Indian tribe live on a reservation in northeastern Wisconsin. Some Menominee live beside their non-Indian neighbors in cities and towns throughout the United States. In all there are about eight thousand Menominee living in the United States.

The name Menominee comes from the word Manoominii, which means "people of the wild rice." The Ojibwa used this term because wild rice was the Menominee's main food. Menominee call themselves Mamaceqtaw (ma-ma-CHAY-tua). It means "the people who live with the seasons."

Thousands of years ago, large sheets of ice called glaciers covered much of the land. People probably crossed a land bridge from Asia to North America. Over time some of the people moved south in search of food and warmer places to live. Among them were **ancestors** of the Menominee. These ancestors settled

This map shows the traditional homeland of the Menominee people.

near the Great Lakes ten thousand years ago. They made tools out of copper that they found in present-day Wisconsin and the Upper Peninsula of Michigan around Lake Superior.

The Menominee grew into a strong Native American group with skilled warriors. They lived as hunters and fishers in the heavily forested region. They gathered wild rice that grew in shallow waters near the shore. The Menominee also planted crops such as corn, beans, and squash. They moved often, gathering fruit, nuts, and roots for food.

The Menominee first met Europeans in 1634, when Jean Nicolet passed through Menominee lands. Nicolet was a French fur trader who was on his way to trade with the Winnebago Indians near present-day Green Bay, Wisconsin. Gradually more French traders arrived in the Great Lakes region. Soon the fur trade was a booming industry. The Menominee traded beaver furs for European goods such as cloth, flour, coffee, sugar, and tools. The French built trading posts where Europeans and Native Americans could exchange goods without using money. The Menominee built villages near the trading posts.

Missionaries arrived and built schools near the villages. They taught Native Americans, including the Menominee, Christian beliefs.

The French and Menominee respected one another and became friends. French traders often married Menominee women. These marriages helped strengthen the friendship between the French and the Menominee. The French had claimed ownership of the Great Lakes region. But in the late

The Menominee and Jean Nicolet first met along the shore of Lake Michigan when the fur trader reached the region in 1634.

1600s, the British, who had also been trading in the area for many years, grew more powerful. The French and British were at war in Europe, and in 1754 the conflict extended to North America, where the two countries fought over territory. This conflict is usually called the French and Indian War. The Menominee and other Native Americans sided with the French. When the British won the war in 1763, they took control of the region.

Traders and Native Americans exchanged goods peacefully throughout much of the 1700s.

In 1776 the American colonies declared their independence from Great Britain. The Menominee supported the British, who eventually lost the war. The Great Lakes region came under American control, but some British remained in the area. The United States and Great Britain fought each other again in the War of 1812 (1812–1815). After the United States won the war, the rest of the British were driven out of the area. The Menominee came under the control of the U.S. government.

Meanwhile Americans were moving west in increasing numbers. They settled on Native American lands and established farms. In 1816 the U.S. government sent a representative to meet with the Menominee near the present-day Mackinaw Bridge in Michigan. Future meetings resulted in **treaties** between the U.S. government and the Menominee. The Menominee did not go to war against the U.S. government, as many Native American groups did. But they did resist the government by delaying meetings between government representatives and Menominee leaders. The Menominee used these delays to stall the U.S. government and stay on their lands.

Between 1817 and 1854, however, the Menominee signed seven major treaties with the United States. The Menominee gave up a total of 9.5 million acres (3.8 million hectares) of land. In return, they received medical care, education, and supplies such as food, farming tools, blankets, salt, and tobacco. In 1854, after the last treaty was signed, the Menominee moved onto a reservation of 234,000 acres (94,700 ha).

Once they moved to the reservation, the Menominee made a living through forestry, which had always been part of their daily lives. Menominee are skilled foresters—people who are trained to plant, care for, and cut down trees. The Menominee built a sawmill to turn the trees they cut down into lumber. Then they sold the lumber. By 1871 their lumber business earned $10,000 a year. In the 1890s **profits** grew to $200,000 per year. The Menominee used the money to build schools and a hospital on the reservation. By the 1940s the sawmill was so successful that the Menominee added a health clinic, a police department, a court system, and a fund to help poor members of the tribe.

At the Menominee's sawmill, logs are carried up the sloped board. Then the round saw blades cut them into boards.

By 1954 the Menominee had shown that they could support themselves. That year the U.S. Congress passed the Menominee Termination Act. This law was passed to end U.S. government protection and support of the Menominee. The reservation became Menominee County, in the state of Wisconsin. The Menominee were no longer recognized as a Native American tribe. The law was a disaster for the Menominee. The tribe's hospital and health clinic had to be closed because they did not meet the standards set by Wisconsin's state government. The sawmill did not make enough money for the Menominee to pay their state taxes. In an effort to make money to pay the taxes, Menominee lands were set aside to be sold so vacation homes could be built for visitors to the region.

The loss of land angered many Menominee. They formed a group called Determination of Rights and Unity for Menominee Shareholders (DRUMS). Their goal was to get Menominee County turned back into a tribal reservation. They also wanted to have the Menominee recognized as a Native American tribe again. DRUMS gained the support of Wisconsin's senators and representatives in Congress, as well as the state's governor. In 1973 President Richard Nixon signed the Menominee Restoration Act. The act gave the county back to the Menominee as a reservation. The Menominee regained recognition as a Native American tribe.

In the years since then the Menominee set up a tribal government, elected leaders, and wrote a constitution. The nation has worked to improve education, health care, and employment opportunities for its people.

Chief Oshkosh

Oshkosh (1795–1858) followed in the footsteps of his father and grandfather as chief of the Menominee. His name means "Claw," but he was often called "The Brave." Oshkosh became chief in 1827. In 1854 he was the leader of more than one hundred families living along the Wisconsin River. Twelve years later he led the families in their move to the reservation. He represented his people in all but one of the treaties signed with the U.S. government. His efforts ensured that the government treated the Menominee fairly. Oshkosh died on August 29, 1858, in Keshena, Wisconsin. The Wisconsin city of Oshkosh is named in his honor. He is buried there in Menominee Park, under a monument dedicated to him.

Chief Oshkosh

2 · LIFE IN THE WOODLANDS

The area where the Menominee lived was mostly forest, or woodlands. The Menominee were Eastern Woodland Indians. Eastern Woodland Indians lived in the region from Minnesota south to the Ohio River and east to the Atlantic Ocean. Tribes spoke one of the Algonquian languages. They lived by hunting, fishing, gathering food, and growing corn, beans, and squash.

The Menominee lived in two different kinds of houses: a summer house and a winter house. During summer they lived in rectangular lodges made of tree bark held together by young trees called saplings. Dome-shaped winter homes were called wigwams. A wigwam was made by bending saplings into a U shape and covering them with bark or reeds. The Menominee may have slept on raised wooden platforms covered with mats made of reeds.

The Menominee were organized into family groups called

This area of forestland in Wisconsin is part of the vast region where the Eastern Woodland Indians lived.

A reconstructed Menominee wigwam near present-day Green Bay, Wisconsin

clans. There were five clans: Bear, Eagle (sometimes called Thunderbird), Wolf, Crane, and Moose. Each clan was divided into thirty-four smaller groups. Each clan had certain jobs. Members of the Eagle clan served the people like modern-day police officers do. During peacetime the leaders were from the Bear clan. During wartime the leaders came from the Eagle clan.

The woodlands provided many different kinds of food. The Menominee hunted in groups for large animals such as bears, deer, and moose. They used traps to catch small animals such as rabbits, squirrels, beavers, and porcupines. The Menominee also ate ducks, geese, and other **waterfowl**. Rivers and lakes provided the Menominee with sturgeon, trout, bass, walleye, perch, and other fish. Fishers caught

Menominee fishers spear salmon by torchlight from birch-bark canoes.

them by spearing the fish from canoes or riverbanks, or by catching them in large nets. The forests also provided berries and fruits, such as apples.

Before the arrival of Europeans, Menominee men may have had more than one wife at the same time. Marriages were arranged by parents, but usually only after a young man and young woman expressed interest in one another. After the couple's families exchanged gifts, the couple was considered married. Once married, a woman moved into her husband's home. Men were the leaders of their families.

When babies were born, their mothers kept them close at all times. Before babies learned to walk, they were strapped onto cradleboards and carried on their mothers' backs. Children who behaved poorly were not usually spanked or scolded. They were convinced to behave by being told that if they were not good a ghost or spirit would take them away while they slept.

Children learned the Menominee way of life by watching and helping adults. Boys hunted and fished with their fathers.

Wild Rice and Maple Syrup

In fall women were usually responsible for gathering wild rice, a kind of grass. They paddled birch-bark canoes through the grass that grew in shallow waters along the shore. They knocked the ripe grains into their boats. When they arrived back onshore, they placed the rice on animal skins to dry. The outer covering, called chaff, was pounded off because it is not good to eat. The grain that was left behind was either used right away or stored for later use.

During early spring the Menominee tapped maple trees for sap to make syrup. The Menominee called sugar maples *michtan*. When the bark of a sugar maple was cut, sap flowed out into baskets that the Menominee attached to the trees. When the sap was boiled, it turned into a thick, sugary syrup. The syrup was used to flavor food. Hardened syrup was candy for Menominee with a sweet tooth.

Native Americans collecting sap to make maple sugar

Men were also responsible for making weapons, tools, canoes, nets, and traps. Boys learned these skills by helping their fathers. Girls helped their mothers tend crops, collect wild plants for food, gather firewood, and carry water. Women also made the clothing, household tools, and pottery. They wove mats and baskets. They taught the girls these skills.

Before contact with Europeans, Menominee men wore **breechcloths** and women wore skirts made of animal skins. Deerskin leggings were worn for warmth in winter and for protection against heavy brush and thorns during summer. In summertime Menominee went barefoot. In winter they wore deerskin moccasins. Winter in the woodlands can be bitterly cold. So the Menominee wore robes and hoods made of bearskin with the fur side in to keep warm. After the arrival of Europeans, the Menominee used blankets they gained in trade. Men wore trousers and shirts and women wore dresses, skirts, and blouses.

The Menominee decorated their clothing with colorful geometric patterns in red, yellow, blue, and black. They also

This photograph of a Menominee family outside their lodge was taken in 1900.

Popped Wild Rice

Wild rice was the most important food in the Menominee diet. This recipe comes from *The Menominee*, by Verna Fowler (see Find Out More on page 45). Be sure to wash your hands with soap and water before you begin. Ask an adult to help you prepare this recipe.

Ingredients

- $^{1}/_{4}$ cup (60 milliliters) wild rice
- 1 tablespoon (15 ml) vegetable oil
- salt (optional)

Rinse the wild rice under cold water thoroughly, several times. Let it dry on a towel overnight, or put it in a warm oven for a short time. Heat the oil in a pot to 375 °F (190°C). Drop the rice by large spoonfuls into the oil. Put a cover on the pot. Hold the pot over the heat, and shake it until the popping stops. Drain on a paper towel. Salt lightly, if needed. When done, the rice will look like puffed cereal.

used shells, feathers, and porcupine quills to decorate the clothing. After the arrival of Europeans, the Menominee used glass beads, cloth fabric, and ribbons as decoration. They became experts in beadwork patterns that looked like flowers. Before and after the arrival of Europeans, Menominee women used grasses and tree bark to weave baskets. The baskets were used for everything from food storage to carrying water.

Menominee men and women grew their hair long. Men wore deer fur and eagle feathers in their hair. Some men wore fur headdresses. During ceremonies some men wore deerskin capes. Men who were participating in ceremonies covered their bodies in grease made from animal fat and put oil in their hair. They also painted religious symbols on their bodies.

Painted Clay Pots

The Menominee made pottery for cooking and food storage. You can decorate your own clay pot.

You will need:

* Brown paper bag
* Clay pot (Clay pots come in a variety of sizes. You can buy one at any craft or hobby store.)
* Paintbrushes
* Paints in any colors you choose
* Pencil (optional)

1. Cut the brown paper bag along one side. Cut off the bottom. Spread the bag flat on your work surface to protect the surface from spills.

2. Paint your clay pot. Decorate it with pictures and symbols that are meaningful to you. Do you like to fish? Paint fish on your pot. Do you have a pet dog, cat, or bird? Paint a picture of your pet. Be creative. You can paint any animal, person, or thing on your pot. You may find it helpful to draw pictures on your pot in pencil first, then paint over them.

3. When you are finished painting your pot, allow it to dry. This may take several hours. Be sure to clean your paintbrushes and store your paints properly, so you can use them on other projects—or maybe to paint another pot.

Show your decorated clay pot to others and share what you have learned about the Menominee.

The Menominee believed in Mecawetok (ma-jen-a-WAY-tuck). Also called Great Spirit, Mecawetok created the earth, the sun, and the stars. The Menominee also believed there was a constant struggle between good and evil. Good spirits lived on four levels above the earth. Evil spirits lived on four levels below the earth. Mecawetok lived at the highest level above the earth. Below him at each level were Thunderbirds (also called Thunderers), the gods of war, and the Morning Star. At the lowest level below the earth was Great White Bear. Great White Bear was the main source of evil. Other evil spirits under the earth were Underground Panther, White Deer, and Horned Hairy Serpent. Horned Hairy Serpent lived in lakes, streams, and rivers. It tried to tip over boats and drag people to the underworld.

The Menominee believed that spirits also lived in the world

The Menominee believed that spirits lived in the sky, the land, and the waters.

around them, not just above and below the earth. The land, rivers, forests, and plants contained spirits. So did the sun, moon, and stars. The spirits had powers that could help or hurt the Menominee. In order to receive the spirits' help, the Menominee used prayers, dances, offerings, and songs to please them. Births, marriages, and deaths were marked by ceremonies to give thanks to the spirits. Menominee hunters and warriors prayed to the spirits for success in hunting and in battle. The Menominee also asked for the spirits' help with planting, harvesting, and food gathering.

The Menominee believed that some individuals called shamans had special powers. A shaman was a kind of priest who used magic to see the unknown, to control events, or to heal the sick. Shamans who healed illnesses were called "medicine men" or "medicine women" by Native Americans. Some shamans received their power during a vision quest. Vision quests were rites of passage in which a Menominee boy or girl painted his or her face black and entered a small wigwam. The youth did not eat or drink for several days,

A Menominee medicine man prepares medicine while holding a gourd rattle and chanting a prayer.

while seeking guidance from the spirit world. Spirits were believed to offer guidance through dreams. After the experience, the youth would tell a shaman about his or her dreams. The shaman told the youth what the dreams meant. The dreams were said to be messages from the spirits, providing rules for the youth to live by during his or her life.

All religious practices included dances. Important dances included the Dream Dance (also called the Drum Dance), in which the Menominee asked for the spirits' help with everyday activities. The Warrior's Dance protected men during warfare.

Illness was believed to be caused by evil spirits. Evil spirits were thought to make people lose their souls. Shamans performed a **ritual** to convince the soul to return. When the soul returned, it entered a small basket. The shaman took the basket to the sick person's relatives. The relatives placed the basket on the sick person's chest for four days so the soul could reenter the body. When the person became well again, it was said to be because the soul had reentered the body.

When a Menominee died, family members painted the body red to symbolize happiness that the person's soul was going to the afterlife. The body was placed on a wooden **platform** or buried in the ground, under logs. Some of the dead person's favorite possessions, such as weapons, tools, and

The Menominee sometimes used burial platforms similar to this one, and placed some of the dead person's favorite belongings with the body.

ornaments, were placed with the body. Ghosts of the dead were believed to stay behind near the body. Menominee feared ghosts, but they visited the gravesite to make food offerings and to play games. Food and games were believed to keep the ghosts happy.

Most modern Menominee are Christian, mainly Catholic. Some combine Christian beliefs with traditional ones. Christian beliefs led the Menominee to celebrate marriages and christenings in churches. An example of combining Christian beliefs and traditional ones is the Menominee practice of burying the dead in coffins under the ground. However, small houselike structures are built above the graves. Food and other offerings for the dead person's soul are placed in openings in the structures.

How the Menominee Came to Be

Mecawetok made the sun, the stars, and Mother Earth. Mother Earth gave birth to Keso (the moon). Keso gave birth to twins. The twins' job was to finish creating the world. The twins made the land, rivers, mountains, lakes, and seas. They also made plants and animals. After they were finished, a great bear rose from the ground beside the present-day Menominee River. As the bear roamed over the land, Mecawetok changed it into a person. This bear became the first Menominee.

While walking beside the river, the first Menominee saw an eagle flying in the sky. The man asked the eagle to be his brother. As the bird flew down to join the man, Mecawetok changed it into the second Menominee.

As the two brothers walked along, they invited a beaver, a sturgeon, an elk, a crane, a wolf, a dog, and a deer to join them. When the animals said yes, they, too, were changed into Menominee. The eldest brothers, bear and eagle, became the tribe's major clans.

Eagles like this one represent one of the Menominee's major clans.

4 · A CHANGING WORLD

The Menominee Indian Reservation covers more than 235,000 acres (95,000 ha) in Wisconsin. The Menominee are proud that their reservation is located in their traditional homeland. The reservation is just 60 miles (97 kilometers) west of the Menominee River, the place where the Menominee believe they were created.

About half of the eight thousand Menominee in the United States live on the Menominee reservation. The reservation is divided into five main villages: Middle Village, Neopit, South Branch, Zoar, and Keshena. Many Menominee who have returned to the reservation after living in other cities and towns in the United States live in Middle Village. A home for older Menominee who need special care is also located in Middle Village. The tribe's sawmill, a Catholic church, two schools, and two grocery stores are located in Neopit. South

The Menominee painted this rock on their reservation in Wisconsin.

The College of Menominee Nation opened in Keshena in 1992.

Branch and Zoar consist of homes, stores, a church, and a building for community gatherings. The tribal headquarters is located in Keshena. Office buildings, stores, a Catholic church, an elementary school, a high school, and the College of Menominee Nation are also located in Keshena. Keshena is home to a large hotel, two casinos, and a bingo hall. The money from these successful businesses helps support the tribe and its people.

The Menominee are governed by a tribal **legislature** made up of nine members. A chairperson is the leader of the legislature. Members are elected in January. They serve three-year terms. The tribe has its own court system and police department. There are separate organizations that oversee businesses, such as the casinos and the sawmill.

The Menominee have two separate school systems. The Menominee Tribal School is in Neopit. Children in kindergarten through eighth grade can attend this school. The Menominee Indian School District is located in Keshena. This is a public school system for Indian and non-Indian children in elementary school through high school.

The College of Menominee Nation opened in 1992. About six hundred Indian and non-Indian students are enrolled in this two-year college. Some students who graduate from this college enter the workforce. Others transfer to four-year colleges in Wisconsin or other states.

The Menominee sawmill still makes lumber. The lumber is shipped all over the world to be used in construction and furniture making. The Menominee also built a factory where they can make lumber into furniture and wood products. The sawmill, factory, stores, schools, casinos, and other businesses provide jobs and income for Menominee workers.

Tourism is another important part of the Menominee economy. The reservation is rich in natural beauty, with its forests, rivers, and lakes. Legend Lake and Bass Lake are especially popular sites for swimming, boating, waterskiing, and fishing. Visitors also enjoy rafting down the Wolf River near Neopit and Middle Village. The Logging Museum of the Menominee Nation is located along the Wolf River. It is the largest museum in the world dedicated to the history of the logging industry. The museum is a **replica** of a logging camp in the 1800s. Seven log buildings contain historic logging artifacts. The Menominee Indian Cultural Museum in Keshena preserves the rich heritage of the Menominee for visitors from all over the country and the world.

Ada Deer

Ada Deer is a well-known Menominee leader. Born in 1935, she was the first Menominee to graduate from the University of Wisconsin–Madison. In the 1970s she worked to restore U.S. government recognition of the Menominee as an Indian tribe. She served as head of the Bureau of Indian Affairs from 1993 to 1997. This U.S. government agency manages more than 87,000 square miles (225,000 square kilometers) of land held by Native Americans. The bureau also provides education services to about 50,000 Native Americans. Ada Deer was the first Native American woman to head the bureau. In January 2000 she became the director of the American Indian Studies program at the University of Wisconsin–Madison.

Ada Deer

In 2006 the Menominee purchased a greyhound-racing track in Kenosha, Wisconsin. They reopened it as a gambling and entertainment site. In the early 2000s Wisconsin Indian groups, including the Menominee, ranked fifth in the nation in the amount of money they earn from their casinos.

Every summer the Menominee Nation Contest Powwow takes place in Keshena. Traditional songs and dances are performed. Tribal arts and crafts are displayed. Contests include a walk/run and youth Olympics. Although most Menominee have a lifestyle similar to that of other Americans, this gathering is a chance to embrace their ancient traditions while living in the modern world.

Native American groups from throughout the Midwest attend the annual Menominee powwow.

TIME LINE

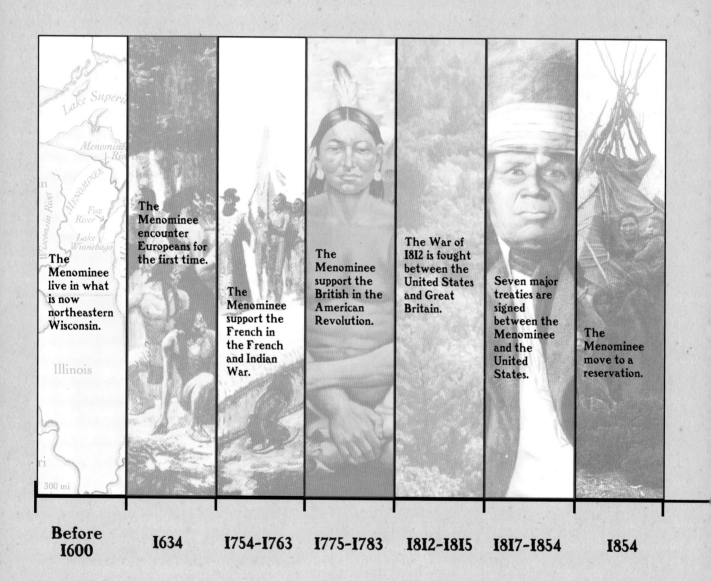

Before 1600	1634	1754–1763	1775–1783	1812–1815	1817–1854	1854

The Menominee live in what is now northeastern Wisconsin.

The Menominee encounter Europeans for the first time.

The Menominee support the French in the French and Indian War.

The Menominee support the British in the American Revolution.

The War of 1812 is fought between the United States and Great Britain.

Seven major treaties are signed between the Menominee and the United States.

The Menominee move to a reservation.

The Menominee sawmill earns $10,000 a year.

1871

Profits from the Menominee sawmill reach $200,000 per year.

1890s

The Menominee lumber business continues to prosper.

1940s

The U.S. Congress passes the Menominee Termination Act.

1954

President Nixon signs the Menominee Restoration Act.

1973

College of Menominee Nation opens.

1992

The Menominee purchase a greyhound-racing track in Kenosha, Wisconsin.

2006

Wisconsin

Iowa

Missouri

Wisconsin River

· GLOSSARY

ancestors: Family members who lived a long time ago.

breechcloths: Simple garments worn by men that reach from the waist to the upper thigh.

legislature: Lawmaking body or council.

missionaries: People who try to convert others to a religion.

platform: A flat, raised structure where people stand or lie down.

profits: Money earned by a business or individual.

replica: An exact copy of an object.

ritual: An action that is always performed in the same way as part of a religious ceremony or social custom.

treaties: Formal, written agreements made between countries or governments.

waterfowl: Swimming birds that are hunted for food.

· FIND OUT MORE

Books

Fowler, Verna. *The Menominee*. Austin, TX: Raintree Steck-Vaughn, 2001.

Lurie, Nancy Oestreich. *Wisconsin Indians*. Madison, WI: Wisconsin Historical Society, 2002.

Smithyman, Kathryn and Bobbie Kalman. *Nations of the Western Great Lakes*. New York: Crabtree Publishing, 2002.

Websites

The Logging Museum of the Menominee Nation
www.menominee-nsn.gov/tourism/logMuseum/museum.php

The Menominee Indian Tribe of Wisconsin
www.menominee-nsn.gov

National Museum of the American Indian
www.nmai.si.edu

Native American Facts for Kids: Menominee Tribe
www.bigorrin.org/menominee_kids.htm

NativeTech
www.nativetech.org

About the Author

Sarah De Capua is the author of many books, including biographical, geographical, historical, and civics titles. She has always been fascinated by the earliest inhabitants of North America. In this series, she has also written *The Iroquois*, *The Cherokee*, *The Cheyenne*, *The Comanche*, *The Shawnee*, *The Shoshone*, and *The Tlingit*. Born and raised in Connecticut, she resides in Georgia.

INDEX

Page numbers in **boldface** are illustrations.